REAL INVESTING

For The Average Joe

Kathy Rex

Copyright © 2023 by Kathy Rex

All rights reserved, including the right to reproduce this book or portions thereof in any form whatsoever or by any means. No part of this book may be reproduced, stored in a retrieval system, or transmitted by any means without the written permission of the Author, except as provided by United States of America copyright law.

First Paperback edition July, 2023

Manufactured in the United States of America

Published by Victory Vision
Publishing and Consulting, LLC
www.victoryvision.org

ISBN: 979-8-9884107-0-6 (paperback)
ISBN: 979-8-9884107-1-3 (eBook)

DEDICATION

To my wonderful children,
Kobi, Kaci, and Kyle,
Follow your dreams,
and be kind to each other.

I love you, always,

Mom/KR

ACKNOWLEDGEMENT

I want to thank the following three individuals for their wonderful teachings and whose ideas, merged together, are the foundation of this book.

Jaspreet Singh, "The Minority Mindset"

Dave Ramsey, "The Dave Ramsey Show"

Jay Garvens, "The Jay Garvens Show"

From their YouTube videos, books, and radio shows, I have taken the principles learned and put them to work in real estate investing.

We started with a net worth of about $200,000 in 2017. Now, just five short years later, our 2022 net worth is well over $2 million. We had been unsuccessful the first 55 years of our lives, trying to invest in the stock market, mutual funds, and insurance. This time we wanted to invest in non-paper assets, something we could see, touch, and most of all, something which would eventually generate income for us.

I wrote this book so anyone with minimum experience—but with the discipline to live below their means and put their money to work for them—can have the same real estate success!

The fourth person who was key to our success was my husband, Steve Rex. He believed in my dreams and supported me every step along the way! Together, we created the future we knew was available to all who trusted and followed simple success principles.

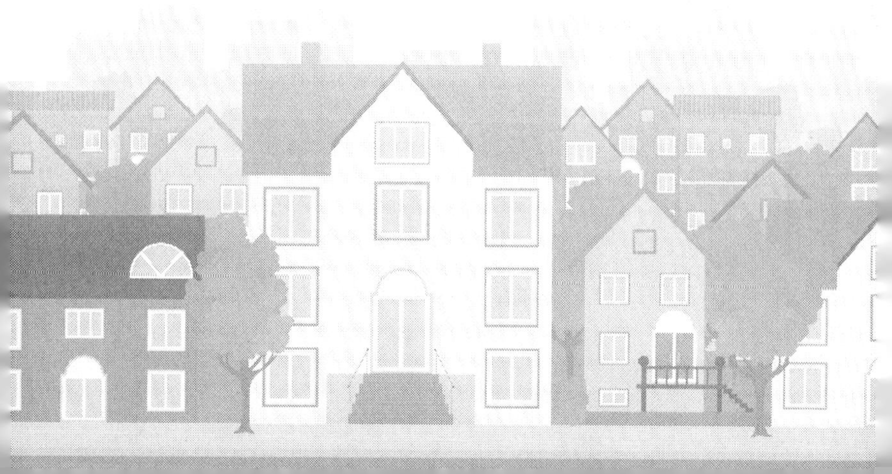

TABLE OF CONTENTS

ix	Introduction
1	Chapter 1: Get Rid of Debt
7	Chapter 2: Purchase Your First Home
17	Chapter 3: Convert Home #1 to Rental, Purchase Home #2 **Focus:** Setting up your First Rental Property
27	Chapter 4: Convert Home #2 to Rental, Purchase Home #3 **Focus:** Tax Benefits & Record Keeping
37	Chapter 5: Convert Home #3 into a Rental Property and Purchase Your Family Home **Focus:** Desires of Today's Home Buyer
41	Chapter 6: Focus on Paying off one Home at a Time
47	Appendix A: Potential Accelerators
51	Appendix B: Helpful Resources
54	Appendix C: Sample Schedule E
55	Glossary
59	About the Author

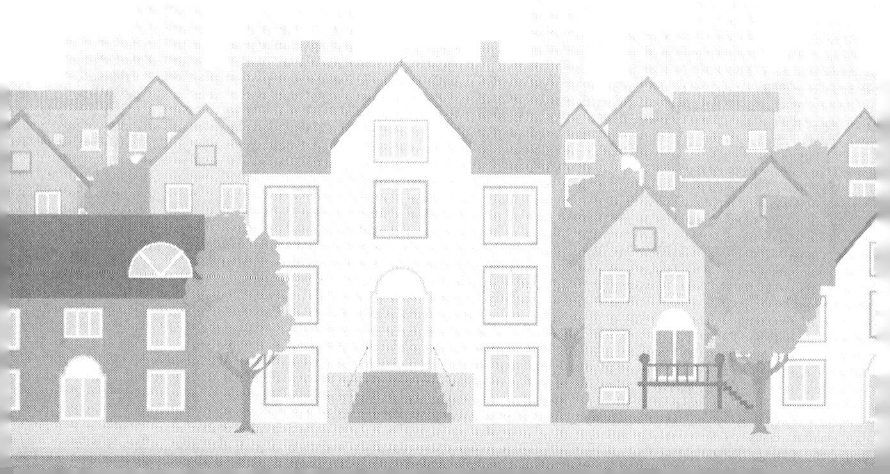

INTRODUCTION

My plan to financial freedom through real estate is simple and attainable by all. In the next few chapters, I will detail each step we followed. Here is the bird's eye view of the plan; the exact details will vary from person to person. Basic success principles never fail, and the real estate market has continued to average 3-5% appreciation over the past 50 years. There have been a few years outside of this norm, but the overall trend will continue.

Step 1: Get rid of all unsecured debt and bring your balance sheet back to even

Step 2: Purchase your first home (3 bedrooms, 2 bathrooms, at least a 1 car garage)

Step 3: Turn home #1 into an investment property, purchase home #2 and move in

Step 4: Turn home #2 into an investment property, purchase home #3 and move in

Step 5: Turn home #3 into an investment property, purchase the perfect home for your family

Step 6: Focus on paying off one home at a time

Step 7: Enjoy the earnings from the three properties and live free of any mortgage payments

CHAPTER 1

GET RID OF DEBT

Our journey started by digging ourselves out of a pool of debt and getting back to even through debt consolidation. Only then, could we actually begin to build wealth for our family. Between credit cards and automobile debt, we had dug a pretty big hole. Through a focused effort, to live below our means, we were able to get back to even in 10 years. We finally figured out that if we spent less than we made each month, we could do it. Our monthly budget meetings kept us on track. Each month we reviewed the results of the previous month and made a plan for exactly where every dollar would go the next month. The final piece of the puzzle was having an emergency fund, not a credit card, for the unexpected needs. Life on planet earth is full of surprises and you just want to be prepared.

Ten years seemed like a lifetime, but we were raising three amazing teenage boys, and wanted to provide a quality life for them at the same time. We had fun family vacations but kept them within our budget. They participated in athletics and learned valuable life lessons. They watched us serve those around us, while simultaneously pursuing our dreams.

Our first step to consolidate debt was to sell our home and use the proceeds to help pay off a few items. We found a beautiful home to rent at a lower cost each month, and were no longer putting funds towards unexpected repairs or improvements. It was a wonderful home and our side business (or side *hustle*, per Jaspreet!) even helped us pay some of the rent. Our business rented a small portion of the basement for its office and storage space. This was extra money we could put towards debt reduction!

If you currently own a smaller home with a mortgage payment very similar to rent payments in your area, I would seek financial advice from your accountant on whether selling makes sense in your situation. The tax advantages and the opportunity to keep your current home may make sense. You will be able to skip the step of purchasing your first home. But be sure to get debt free and have established a fully funded emergency fund before you convert the home to an investment property.

For your debt consolidation, I highly recommend following Dave Ramsey's first three Baby Steps:

> **Baby Step 1** – Save $1,000 for your starter emergency fund
>
> **Baby Step 2** – Pay off all debt using the "Debt Snowball" method
>
> **Baby Step 3** – Save 3-6 months of expenses in a fully funded emergency fund

We followed Dave Ramsey's "Debt Snowball" method exactly. Please read one of Dave Ramsey's books which goes through the method in detail. We attacked our debts with gazelle-like intensity!

We sold our vehicles which had larger payments, and used the proceeds to purchase safe, inexpensive cars. We were able to purchase one of the used vehicles with cash. For our second car, we had to finance the purchase, but we were able to secure a much smaller monthly payment. My husband was crushed when he had to turn in his beautiful four-wheel drive Audi for a no-frills Honda Civic, to go with our used, family-friendly Chrysler mini-van. When you face similar emotions in this process, keep coming back to the long-term payoffs; in retrospect, these changes were small prices to pay for the gains we made.

Each time we paid off a debt we had a small celebration. By the time we were debt-free, we just wanted to keep the focus and decided to put our celebration funds towards our fully funded emergency account.

When it came time for college, we promised to help our boys with $5,000/semester if they maintained good grades. The rest of the cost was up to them. Our first son went to Harvard for a year before deciding to attend the U.S. Air Force Academy. Our second son went to Northwestern Prep School for one semester, Pikes Peak Community College for the second semester, and then attended the U.S. Coast Guard Academy. Our third son attended our local university on a full-ride scholarship his first year. For the remaining time, to earn his degree, he worked part-time to help with his share of the expense. All three sons are well on their way to prosperous careers and have minimal or no revolving or student loan debt.

Once you are debt free, keep just **one credit card** to use and pay off each month. Do not close any credit card accounts, just cut the cards and never use them again as you pay them off. You must be fully committed to paying this credit card off each month. Every dollar spent on this card should be part of your monthly plan, so it is easy to pay off at the end of each month. For example, we used the credit card for just our gas to fuel our vehicles. All other expenses were paid with cash or with our debit card. By maintaining one credit card, your credit score will remain high. And with no debt, your credit score should remain very high every month, and this will be very helpful as you begin to purchase homes.

"Be sure to get debt free and have established a fully funded emergency fund before you convert the home to an investment property."

CHAPTER 2

PURCHASE YOUR FIRST HOME

Now that you have mastered spending less than you make each month, it is time to put your money to work! The next step is to save up enough money for a down payment on your first home. You will move into this home, and it will be your primary residence for a minimum of one year. You will live in the home until you are able to save up enough money for your next down payment, the purchase of home #2.

There are several benefits to purchasing a home as a primary residence:

- Lower down payment required
- Lowest mortgage interest rate
- Lowest mortgage insurance, if using a conventional loan
- No added government fees

WHAT TYPE OF HOME SHOULD I PURCHASE?

Before your even begin to look at homes, you will need to find a quality real estate agent. I recommend interviewing at least two agents and have them share why you should work with them. After the interviews, I would call a few of their past clients and/or research their online survey results. Experience in investment property purchases is key. An agent with a nice portfolio of investment homes themselves can be quite helpful. They are a wealth of knowledge based on their past experiences and will also have a team of service professionals who can assist with property management, home inspections, repairs, accounting, and legal assistance.

This first home will eventually become rental home #1. You are looking for a home your family will be happy to live in for two years and will make a nice rental property. From past experience, I have found the best rental property will be a 3-bedroom, 2-bathroom, single family home or townhome, with at least a 1-car garage. This size home is perfect for a small family or older couple, my favorite renters. The optimum square footage is between 1200 to 1800 sq. ft. A small yard area is a suggested feature, with just a few smaller trees (if any) and a small grass area.

Here are the pros and cons of purchasing a single-family home vs. a townhome.

	Single Family	**Townhome**
Pros	Space from neighbors	Outside maintenance provided
	Minimal HOA fees or rules	Reduced insurance & taxes
Cons	You or your tenant must maintain the yard	HOA fees & rental rules
	Higher purchase price, taxes & insurance	Often slower to appreciate

The location of your home is very important. Find a desirable area in town with a quality school system. Do not be on a busy street or back up to one. It is beneficial to have easy access to the highway, parks, grocery shopping and restaurants. If purchasing a townhome, an end unit or a unit with some outside space with privacy is vital. I would not purchase a brand-new home. Look for an existing home with simple but attractive landscaping and blinds/window coverings provided.

HOW MUCH SHOULD YOU SPEND ON AN INVESTMENT PROPERTY?

A great rule of thumb for purchasing an investment property is to not spend more than four times the local area's median income. For example, in Colorado Springs the area median income is $96,200. The optimal purchase price for your investment property should be no more than four times this amount, or $384,800.

To find the median income for your area, you can go to:

https://ami-lookup-tool.fanniemae.com/amilookuptool/

FINANCING YOUR PROPERTY

There are three needed financial items when purchasing a home:

1. A strong **credit score**: 740 or higher is recommended. This will get you an optimum rate and the lowest monthly mortgage insurance.
2. Solid **income** in the same career field for the past two years.
   a. W-2 Wage Earners, box 5 on your W2 is your income used for calculations.
   b. Self-employed borrowers using a Schedule C on their tax return, your Net Profit is used for the calculations. Gross income less expenses. (Line 31 on the Schedule C)
   c. Self-employed borrowers filling as an LLC using a 1120S, box 1 on the K-1 (Ordinary Business Income) and your annual distribution (Box 16D on the K-1) will both be considered. The higher of the two will be deemed your business income for the year.

d. Income from Other Sources (these are the most common and must be documented):
     - Social Security Income
     - Alimony
     - Child Support
     - Disability
     - Dividend/Interest
     - Pension
     - Royalties
     - VA Benefits (non-educational)
3. **Assets** (for down payment, closing costs, prepaids and reserves)
   - Checking and Savings Accounts
   - Certificates of Deposit (CD)
   - Cryptocurrency (only if withdrawn)
   - Investment Funds
   - Life Insurance Cash Value
   - Retirement Funds
   - Home Equity Line of Credit (only if withdrawn)

HOW MUCH DOWN PAYMENT WILL YOU NEED?

Plan to put at least 5% down on all purchases. This will vary depending on the loan program you use. In addition, you should plan to pay an additional 2-4% of the purchase price for prepaids and closing costs. Depending on the purchase environment in your market, getting some seller concessions could be very helpful. You can use these funds, from the seller, to help buy down the rate or offset some of the closing costs and/or prepaids. Be sure to ask your real estate agent whether seller concessions are a possibility for your purchase.

Conventional Loans – When using a conventional loan, I recommend putting 5% down. This will allow you to get into the home as quick as possible, while keeping the monthly mortgage insurance to a minimum. Once your loan to value of the home is below 78% or less, the monthly mortgage insurance charge can be removed.

Veteran Administration Loans (VA Loans) – When using a VA loan, you have the benefit of putting $0 down and typically the rate is slightly lower than a conventional rate. If you have a VA disability rating of 10% or more, then you will not have a funding fee.

If you do not have a VA disability rating, then you will be charged a funding fee. This fee is typically added to your loan amount. If you put $0 down and the funding fee is added to your loan, it will definitely take longer to build equity in the home.

Note: If you have used your VA benefit previously to purchase a home and do not have a VA disability rating, I would highly encourage you to plan to put the 5% down and reduce your funding fee by more than half.

WHAT ARE CLOSING COSTS AND PREPAIDS?

Closing costs and prepaids are fees associated with your home purchase. They vary from state to state and vary with the lender you choose. The total for both closing costs and prepaids is roughly 2-4% of the purchase price. For a purchase of $300,000, you can expect to pay a total of $6000 – $12,000.

Standard closing costs:

- Processing & Underwriting
- Appraisal fee
- Title Fees
- State Recording Fees and Transfer Tax

Optional closing costs:

- Origination fees
- Points – charge for a reduced interest rate
- Credit Report
- Document preparation fees

Prepaids costs:

- Prepaid interest, varies depending on the date of the month you close your loan
- 1 year of Homeowner's insurance
- Setup costs for your escrow account (additional 3 months of insurance and 3 months of taxes)
- Any prepaid Home Owner Association (HOA) fees or assessments

I recommend getting preapproved by a local lender prior to your purchase. Contact two lenders recommended by your real estate agent, and get preapproved by both lenders and request a loan estimate from each one. Compare both estimates closely, side by side. Rate is important, but the fees charged will impact the amount of money you will need to bring to closing. A good real estate agent will help you compare the two loan estimates and offer suggestions on the best lender for you. Once you find a lender you like, continue to use the same mortgage loan officer for all your purchases.

CHAPTER 3

CONVERT HOME #1 TO A RENTAL PROPERTY AND PURCHASE HOME #2

Once you have saved enough money for the down payment, closing costs, prepaids and reserve funds required for purchasing a second home, then you are ready to think about purchasing home #2. Again, you will be moving into this new home and renting your current one. All the home purchase parameters from Chapter 2 still apply. It will be a bit easier now that you have one home purchase under your belt. Here are the estimated total funds needed for your purchase of home #2.

- Down payment - 5% of new purchase price
- Closing costs & prepaids – 2-4% of purchase price

- Reserves – 6 months of monthly mortgage payments for both homes

Example: For a purchase of $300,000, here is an estimate of the funds needed:

Down payment	$15,000
Closing Cost & Prepaids	$10,000
*Reserve Estimate	$25,000
Total Needed	$50,000

*Checking, savings, investment funds, retirement funds, and even the cash value on your life insurance are all options for reserve funds. The only way to use funds from a cryptocurrency account or a HELOC is to withdraw the funds into your checking or savings account and have them available for use. In most real estate markets, your emergency funds should cover the needed reserves!

To qualify for the new loan, you will need the big three items again:

- A quality credit score, 740+
- Documentation of the assets mentioned above.

- Sufficient income to keep your DTI (debt to income ratio), below 50%

To offset the mortgage payment on home #1, you will need to have a signed lease and a deposit check. Per most underwriting guidelines, the lease needs to begin at least 60 days after your closing on the purchase of home #2. You can use 75% of the lease amount to offset the mortgage payment of home #1.

Example: Rental contract with lease payment of $2,000/month.

75% of $2,000 = $1,500 to offset the mortgage payment of home #1.

HOW DO I RENT MY FIRST HOME?

To many, renting your own home can seem like a daunting task, but with the help of a quality property manager it can be simplified. The 8-12% fee the best property managers charge is well worth the investment. A good property manager takes care of finding the tenants, qualifying them, collecting the monthly payments, managing timely repairs, and provides assistance if an issue should arise with your tenants.

I like to have all my rental properties within a small radius, in one city or town. I also like to use the same property manager when possible, and that is more feasible when the rentals are all within a close area.

Similar to the selection process of your real estate agent, I recommend interviewing at least two property managers and having them share why you should work with them. After the interviews, call a few of their past clients and/or research their online survey results. Property management experience is key. Experienced property managers have a wealth of knowledge based on their past experiences. Additionally, they will have a quality team of service professionals who can assist with repairs, accounting, periodic visits inside the home, and legal issues, should they arise.

My favorite renters have been young professionals, older couples, or small families. They usually have some home repair knowledge for smaller items, and they have pride in the home. It is important that your property manager has potential renters fill out an application, pulls their credit scores, does an interview, and, most importantly, checks references. The enjoyment of your rental experience is dependent upon the quality of your renter, so choose wisely.

HOW MUCH SHOULD I CHARGE FOR MY RENTAL PROPERTY?

Use the expertise of your real estate agent and property manager to assist you with determining the right price point for your rental home. They can do a market analysis for current rental homes in your area. When determining your monthly lease amount, be sure to consider the following additional items:

- Who will maintain the yard? When possible, I prefer to maintain the yard for my client. I provide the weekly mowing, weed management, and spring and fall clean-ups. The cost of these items I build into the monthly rent. In the past, I have tried to require the renters to maintain the grass. In all cases, good intentions fell short, and I ended up keeping their security deposit to resod the lawn.
- Are pets allowed? If so, will you charge monthly pet rent? Is there an extra pet

deposit required? Based on past experience, I allow for one small dog up to 30 lbs. Absolutely, no cats! I do charge an extra $500 pet deposit and also a $50/month pet rent fee.

- My renters are always responsible for their own utilities, internet, and trash removal, unless provided by the HOA.
- What funds will you collect upon signing the lease? I like to collect a security deposit; the pet deposit (if applicable); and the first and last month of rent.

    Example: Funds due at signing for a $1500/month lease:

First Month's Rent	$1,500
Last Month's Rent	$1,500
Security Deposit	$1,500
Pet Deposit	$ 500
Total Due	$5,000

- Duration of the lease? For quality candidates, I offer a one- or two-year lease with the options to renew annually. If the only option is a weaker qualified renter, I will shorten the lease to 6 months, with the option to renew every six months.

FUNDS MANAGEMENT FOR RENTAL PROPERTY

I recommend opening a checking account specifically for the income and expenses solely related to rental property #1. All rent checks are automatically deposited into this account. All expenses, including the mortgage, are paid from this account. The monthly excess revenue above your mortgage payment will be captured in this account. This positive balance can be used to pay for expenses of rental property #1 and to begin to build a reserve fund. The reserve funds will be used to pay for future long-term maintenance of the property.

Here are a few annual maintenance items we have found very helpful:

- HVAC system – inspect at minimum annually and replace filters quarterly
- Sprinkler system – inspect at minimum annually and in colder areas schedule system startup in spring and blowout in fall

- Pest control – schedule periodically per the needs of your area
- Landscaping – when needed and provide spring and fall cleanup
- Gutters – inspect at minimum annually, if applicable

HOW TO TITLE YOUR INVESTMENT PROPERTY?

Limited Liability Companies (LLCs) are fast becoming a preferred entity type for holding title of investment properties. The major advantage of an LLC is limiting your personal liability should an unforeseen circumstance arise to your property.

For example, if someone is injured while visiting a property you own, even if you do not reside there or have any connection to the guest, they could potentially pursue a legal claim against you, the owner, for your injuries.

On the other hand, if the deed and title to the property is in the name of an LLC, only the LLC (and not you) would be named as defendant. More importantly, only the LLC's assets would be obligated to pay a monetary award and your personal assets are not exposed.

Please contact a legal professional to help you determine if this is the best option for you. All you would need to do is: (1) create the LLC, (2) use a Quit Claim Deed to transfer the title to your LLC, and (3) make sure your rental property bank account is in the LLC's name.

"Experienced property managers have a wealth of knowledge based on their past experiences."

CHAPTER 4

CONVERT HOME #2 TO A RENTAL PROPERTY AND PURCHASE HOME #3

With repetition, we become better at the home purchase and rental process! You will move into home #3 and turn home #2 into your second investment property. The purchase parameters for home #3 will remain the same as mentioned in Chapter 2. The funds needed will be slightly higher this time. The sale price will likely be slightly higher due to home appreciation and your reserve fund needs will be larger to cover 6 months of mortgage payments for all three homes.

Example: For a purchase of $320,000, estimated funds needed are:

Down payment	$16,000
Closing Cost & Prepaids	$11,000
Reserve Estimate	$40,000
Total Needed	$67,000

TAX BENEFITS OF OWNING A RENTAL PROPERTY

By now you have owned your first rental property for more than one year and you will have to file taxes. You will be pleasantly surprised to learn just how friendly the U.S. tax code is to real estate investors. Here are the key tax advantages and deductions for rental property that every real estate investor should know:

1. Operating expenses: funds used for managing and maintaining a rental property are tax deductible. As the IRS explains, ordinary and necessary expenses may include:

    - Advertising costs
    - Leasing commissions
    - Property management fees

- Repairs and maintenance
- Supplies
- Landscaping
- Pest control
- Property taxes
- Homeowner and landlord liability insurance
- Utilities paid directly by the landlord
- Professional service fees, such as an accountant or real estate attorney

2. Mortgage interest: the interest you paid on a loan used to purchase a rental property is fully tax deductible.

3. Depreciation expense: The IRS allows real estate investors to depreciate rental property over a period of 27.5 years to recover the cost of wear and tear. Because land does not wear out, only the cost of the home plus other items that increase the cost basis such as a new roof, appliances, or carpeting may be depreciated.

   To illustrate, let's assume an investor paid $150,000 for a single-family rental home. The lot value is $15,000, which means the cost basis used for depreciation is $135,000. When the home was purchased, the investor replaced the roof at a cost of $20,000 and installed brand new kitchen appliances at a cost of $4,000.

According to the IRS, appliances are depreciated over a period of five years, while the cost of the roof uses the same depreciation period as that of the property.

Here are the steps to follow to calculate the depreciation for the rental property for the first full year of ownership:

1. Add cost of the roof to the property cost basis: $135,000 + $20,000 = $155,000 adjusted cost basis
2. Calculate annual depreciation expense: $155,000 cost basis / 27.5 years = $5,636
3. Calculate appliance depreciation: $4,000 kitchen appliances / 5 years = $800
4. Calculate total depreciation expense: $5,636 + $800 = $6,436

Assuming the rental property in this example generated a pre-tax income of $8,000, an investor could deduct the total depreciation expenses of $6,436 to reduce the amount of taxable income to $1,564.

After five years, the depreciation expense for the appliances would be used up, and the investor's annual depreciation expense would decrease to $5,636, assuming no other capital improvements are made to the property.

4. Section 1031 tax deferred exchange: Defer paying capital gains tax and tax on depreciation recapture by conducting a Section 1031 tax deferred exchange.

Normally, when a rental property is sold, the depreciation expense is recaptured and taxed as ordinary income to an investor, up to a maximum rate of 25% (depending on the investor's federal income tax bracket).

In addition to paying tax on depreciation recapture, an investor also pays a long-term capital gains tax of 0%, 15%, or 20% on any profit from the sale.

With a 1031 exchange, instead of paying taxes, an investor can put the money to work by investing in another rental property. The rules and restrictions relating to a Section 1031 exchange are complex and as an investor, please consult a licensed professional.

Instead of selling rental property, some investors keep their portfolio and draw rental income until eventually passing the property to their heirs. When a property is inherited, the cost basis is stepped up to the current market value of the property, and any outstanding capital gains tax and depreciation recapture tax liability is eliminated for the heir.

5. Owner expenses: Even when a real estate investor hires a local property manager to take care of the tenant and home, there may still be expenses an owner can deduct to reduce taxable income, such as:

   Continuing education - Money spent on dues to belong to a real estate investing club, subscriptions to real estate or business periodicals, and tuition paid for continuing education can normally be deducted from income generated from a rental property business.

Travel - Rental property owners can generally deduct travel expenses, such as airfare and lodging.

- Travel must be mainly for business and have a clear business purpose
- Majority of the time must be spent on business activities and not leisure activities
- Travel expenses must be ordinary and necessary for the real estate business but not be overdone, such as staying a reasonably priced hotel versus a five-star resort
- The standard mileage deduction is the simplest way to deduct business-related travel expenses; the rate varies each year.

6. You avoid FICA taxes: Taxpayers who are self-employed are normally required to pay the employer and employee portion of Social Security and Medicare taxes, also known as FICA or payroll tax. Fortunately, income from a rental property is

usually not classified as earned income, which means the income is not subject to FICA tax.

For example, if the taxpayer owns a business and receives $100,000 in earned annual income, the payroll tax would be 15.3% or $15,300. On the other hand, if the same $100,000 was income generated from rental properties, there would be no FICA tax due.

RECORD KEEPING BEST PRACTICES

In order to profit from the tax benefits of owning a rental property, the IRS requires investors to keep good records. Good records help investors to:

- Monitor rental property performance
- Prepare financial statements
- Identify the source of income and expenses
- Track deductible expenses
- Prepare tax returns

If a tax return is selected for an audit, investors must be able to provide documentary evidence such as receipts, canceled bills or proof of payment, and support for travel expenses. Investors who are unable to provide evidence to support tax deductions may be subject to additional taxes, penalties, and interest.

LENDER'S MONTHLY RENTAL INCOME CALCULATION (ONCE TAXES HAVE BEEN FILED FOR A PROPERTY)

The Schedule E of your tax return is used to report income and loss from your rental properties. When you purchase home #3, your lender will no longer use the lease to offset your mortgage payment on home #1 since you have filed taxes. Instead, your lender will use the numbers as reported on your Schedule E (average of the most recent two years) to calculate your gross income for the property. It is important that you have a quality accountant who puts all expenses into the correct categories on the Schedule E.

The calculation used for numbers shown on the Schedule E, for each property owned, is as follows:

Reported Rent – All Reported Expenses = Reported Income (RI)

RI + Insurance + Taxes + Mortgage Insurance + Depreciation = Gross Annual Income (GAI)

GAI / divided by number of months rented = Gross Monthly Income

"It is important that you have a quality accountant who puts all expenses into the correct categories on the Schedule E."

CHAPTER 5

CONVERT HOME #3 TO RENTAL, PURCHASE YOUR HOME

The time has come to purchase the perfect home for your family! You will follow the same steps outlined in the previous chapters and turn home #3 into an investment property. Once accomplished, you can begin the search for the home you would like to live in long term. You will likely need to save up a bit more for this home, but that is dependent upon the needs and desires of your family. The big question is, how much should you spend on your new home?

I like Dave Ramsey's recommendation of spending no more than 25% of your monthly take-home income on your housing expenses. For housing expenses, be sure to include principal, interest, taxes, homeowner's insurance, and private mortgage insurance (if applicable). Do not forget to include homeowner's association (HOA) fees if your new home or townhome is part of an HOA.

Have fun shopping for **your** home with all the home features **you** would like. Once you move into home #4, the frequent moves are over for a while!! You can finally do all the special touches you have been dreaming of and enjoy them long term.

As you search and plan for the new home, I think it is helpful to keep in mind those home features that the majority of today's home buyers are requesting. Sometimes life can throw us a curve ball, and we end up moving unexpectedly and need to sell quickly. A home with most of the desired features can be helpful. Here are some to consider:

1. Built-in storage throughout the home
   - Kitchen pantry
   - Walk-in closet in master bedroom
   - Garage storage spaces
   - Basement storage with shelving
   - Storage shed in the backyard

2. Updated kitchen
   - Marble, granite, or quartz surfaces
   - Updated appliances
   - Double sinks
   - Kitchen island with built-in seating
   - Plenty of storage
3. Energy Efficiencies
   - Appliances
   - Quality windows with white frames
   - Newer HVAC system
   - Ceiling fans
   - Security system
4. Open layout with separate living spaces
   - Potential home office space
   - Bonus or game room
5. Outdoor living space with exterior lighting
   - Covered patio or deck
   - Covered front porch
   - Small lawn area
6. Hardwood or vinyl plank flooring in common use areas
7. Neutral paint colors throughout
8. Separate Laundry Room
9. Bathroom on the main living floor

"As you search and plan for the new home, I think it is helpful to keep in mind those home features that the majority of today's home buyers are requesting."

CHAPTER 6

FOCUS ON PAYING OFF ONE HOME AT A TIME

With our developed habit of saving each month for the next purchase, we simply redirected those funds to paying off our homes. We began with paying off home #4, our long-term primary residence.

The simplest way to begin paying off our mortgage was to pay extra money each month with our mortgage payment. We started with the most budget-friendly way to pay off a mortgage, by simply paying 1/12 extra each month with our payment. For example, by paying $2,167 each month on a $2000 mortgage payment, we paid the equivalent of an extra payment each year. This method takes 6-7 years off the back end of a 30-year mortgage. Our mortgage freedom point now was 23.5 years.

Due to our ages, my husband and I wanted to focus our efforts and speed up the process. We decided to put all our investment/savings income each month towards paying down our mortgage as quickly as possible. We were saving roughly $2,000 per month and paid that directly towards principal with our monthly mortgage payment. For example, by paying $4,000 each month on a $2000 mortgage payment, our mortgage freedom point was reduced even lower, to roughly 9 years.

To accelerate the mortgage payoff even further, once we had an 80% loan-to-value of our home, we refinanced the balance into an All-in-One loan. This is a home loan that combines a bank account, a mortgage, and a home equity line of credit (HELOC) into one product. This is an interest only, adjustable-rate loan. The rate is usually slightly higher than a fixed rate loan. It is designed to help borrowers who are good at saving each month to pay down their loan quickly and own their home outright. It also provides instant liquidity to your equity for emergencies and for future larger purchases. We like to call it our "Wealth Accumulation Tool"!

We had heard about this product for several years from multiple financial planners, but it took us a while to grasp the concept. We started with baby steps, but once we saw the benefits, we attacked with gazelle-like intensity!

After successfully paying off all our homes, we realized a simple first-position HELOC would have provided the same benefits. The refinance would have cost much less, and the interest rate would have been just slightly higher. Be sure to compare both options before you proceed.

HOW WE USED THE ALL-IN-ONE LOAN:

We refinanced the balance of our mortgage into an All-in-One loan. The first thing we did was to put our fully funded emergency fund into the account to quickly reduce the balance, which in turn reduced our monthly mortgage payment right away. Each month, we put in the same $4000 ($2000 of savings and the $2000 we had been putting into our mortgage payment). When we had extra money in a month, from a bonus, investment payoff, or gift, we put it right towards the balance.

We concentrated our energy further, by cashing out our low performing stocks/mutual funds. By putting our money towards the homes, we were guaranteed to make at least 4-6%, depending on the monthly interest rate.

	Monthly Additions	**Loan Balance**
New All-in-One		$260,000
Initial payment (interest-only at 5%)	$1,083	
Transfer of fully funded emergency fund	-$50,000	$210,000
1st Month		
Deposit (savings + mortgage payment)	-$4,000	$206,000
Extra income (when available) All-in-One monthly payment (New lower balance at 5%)	+$858	$206,858
2nd Month		
Deposit (savings + mortgage payment)	-$4,000	$202,858
Extra income (received $5,000 bonus)	-$5,000	$197,858
All-in-One monthly payment (New lower balance at 5.1%)	+$841	$198,699

3rd Month

Deposit (savings + mortgage payment)	-$4,000	$194,699
Extra income (additional savings)	-$1,000	$193,699
All-in-One monthly payment	+$791	$194,490
(New lower balance at 4.9%)		

4th Month

Deposit (savings + mortgage payment)	-$4,000	$190,490
Extra Income (traded low perform stock)	-$30,000	$160,490
All-in-One monthly payment	+$669	$161,828
(New lower balance at 5%)		

Subsequent Months

Deposit (savings + mortgage payment)	-$4,000	$157,828
Extra Income (when available)	+$658	$158,516
All-in-One Monthly payment		
(New lower balance at 5%)		

The figures show how quickly we were able to pay down our home mortgage. Once the All-in-One loan balance was $5,000 or less, we used the available funds to pay off the loan for investment property #1. Since our emergency fund was part of this loan availability, we would only let the balance go up to $250,000. This left us a reserve of $10,000 for an emergency fund, and we really focused our efforts on paying down the balance quickly to recoup all of our fully funded emergency fund.

We repeated this process for investment property #2 and investment property #3. Today, we have four properties which are completely paid off! Our primary home is mortgage free and the other three properties generate monthly income.

Once the four homes were paid off, we were able to quickly replace our fully funded emergency fund. My husband was able to retire, and I plan to do the same in just 24 months. With the extra money we are still saving each month, we are learning new ways to invest those funds. Who knows, we may even purchase another property, should we find the right home!

APPENDIX A

POTENTIAL ACCELERATORS

In this booklet, I have shared the exact method we used to get financially free with real estate. Here are a few other ideas which I have seen others use which can also help to speed up the process.

PURCHASE A MULTIFAMILY HOME

With the purchase of a duplex, triplex, or quadplex you can acquire multiple properties in one transaction. As long as you move into one of the units, you are able to purchase and count a multi-family home as a primary residence.

If you are a veteran, this is a very interesting option. When using a VA loan, veterans can put $0 down on a multifamily home when occupying one unit as their primary residence. The conforming loan limit also goes up for a multi-family home purchase:

2023 CONFORMING LOAN LIMITS

One-Unit Limit	Two-Unit Limit	Three-Unit Limit	Four-Unit Limit
$ 726,200	$ 929,850	$ 1,123,900	$ 1,396,800

For a conventional loan, the required down payment increases with a multifamily home.

- Duplex – 15% down payment requirement
- 3 or 4 units – 25% down payment requirement

Be sure to consult with your lender to determine if a multifamily home makes sense for you.

REFINANCE TO A LOWER MORTGAGE RATE AND/OR SHORTER TERM

Some investors prefer sticking with a fixed rate loan. When the mortgage interest rates fall significantly, it is wise to consider a refinance. A refinance is recommended when you can reduce your interest rate 1-2% and/or you can shorten the term of your loan. Remember, a refinance comes with closing costs. You should only refinance if you are planning to keep your home long term. By staying in the home several years, you have time for your interest savings to make up for what you paid in closing costs.

SHORT TERM VS. LONG TERM RENTAL

Rental property can be either a short-term or long-term rental:

- Short term rental: Typically rented on a daily, weekly, or monthly basis. Examples of short-term residential rentals include: (1) vacation rental homes, (2) a house hacker who rents out a spare bedroom, and (3) a single-family rental home with a tenant on a month-to-month lease.
- Long term rental: generally rented to a tenant with a 12-month lease term at a fixed annual rent.

For our strategy outlined in this booklet, we used long-term rentals exclusively. We liked the predictable income, lower operating expenses, and minimal turnover.

Some investors like the higher gross income potential and flexibility of a short-term rental.

With a successful short-term rental property, you can generate 2-3 times more each month than a long-term rental. The flexibility of short-term rentals allows the owner to rent the property when vacant and use it themselves when it works well for their schedule.

If you are considering a short-term rental, please consider the following:

- Income is not guaranteed. There is a risk the home will sit vacant for extended periods of time, so work that into your return on investment (ROI) calculation.
- Maintenance is more intensive since the tenant is expecting vacation rental quality. The property will need to be fully furnished and well-maintained, in order to keep your five-star rating.
- As the owner, you will be responsible for all utilities: electricity, gas, water, trash, cable, and internet.
- Many HOA's and cities have strict rules for short-term rental properties. Be sure to carefully read through all HOA documents and check with your city for any additional taxes, fees and/or requirements.

APPENDIX B

HELPFUL RESOURCES

Here are some of the resources we used on our journey to financial freedom through real estate.

Dave Ramsey's Website – Dave's website, www.ramseysolutions.com, is full of helpful tools. Here are the tools we used:

1. Attend a Financial Peace University seminar or course. Hope starts here! https://www.ramseysolutions.com/ramseyplus/financial-peace/financial-peace-university
2. Read his book, "The Total Money Makeover." https://www.ramseysolutions.com/store/books/the-total-money-makeover-by-dave-ramsey

3. Use Ramsey's EveryDollar app to track your budget or go online and find a budgeting tool that fits your needs.

Jaspreet Singh's Website – Visit www.minoritymindset.com and learn about Jaspreet. Here are the benefits of his website:

1. On the homepage of his website, click the "Start Learning" button. This takes you to his Money 101 tab, a FREE Step-by-Step Guide for building wealth. https://theminoritymindset.com/money-101/
2. Watch several of Jaspreet's YouTube videos. He puts out a new video almost every day. You can go into his video library and find the ones that interest you the most.
3. Join *Market Briefs*! A FREE daily financial newsletter which takes only five minutes to read and keeps you educated and entertained. https://briefs.co/

The Jay Garvens Show, "Home Mortgage Talk" – In Jay's witty radio shows he shares his home investing ideas mixed in with news and statistics about the Colorado Springs market.

1. To listen to one of his past episodes, visit https://www.jaygarvens.com/category/episodes/
2. For those of you who live in Colorado Springs area, you can tune in to KRDO News Radio, 1240AM or 105.5FM and listen to his show on Saturday mornings from 8am–9am MST.

APPENDIX C

SAMPLE SCHEDULE E

SCHEDULE E (Form 1040)	Supplemental Income and Loss	OMB No. 1545-0074
Department of the Treasury Internal Revenue Service	(From rental real estate, royalties, partnerships, S corporations, estates, trusts, REMICs, etc.) Attach to Form 1040, 1040-SR, 1040-NR, or 1041. Go to www.irs.gov/ScheduleE for instructions and the latest information.	2022 Attachment Sequence No. 13

Name(s) shown on return | Your social security number

Part I — Income or Loss From Rental Real Estate and Royalties

Note: If you are in the business of renting personal property, use Schedule C. See instructions. If you are an individual, report farm rental income or loss from Form 4835 on page 2, line 40.

A Did you make any payments in 2022 that would require you to file Form(s) 1099? See instructions — Yes / No
B If "Yes," did you or will you file required Form(s) 1099? — Yes / No

1a Physical address of each property (street, city, state, ZIP code)
A
B
C

1b Type of Property (from list below):
A 1
B
C

2 For each rental real estate property listed above, report the number of fair rental and personal use days. Check the QJV box only if you meet the requirements to file as a qualified joint venture. See instructions.

	Fair Rental Days	Personal Use Days	QJV
A	365		
B			
C			

Type of Property:
1 Single Family Residence 3 Vacation/Short-Term Rental 5 Land 7 Self-Rental
2 Multi-Family Residence 4 Commercial 6 Royalties 8 Other (describe)

		Properties:		
		A	B	C
Income:				
3 Rents received	3	22,200		
4 Royalties received	4			
Expenses:				
5 Advertising	5			
6 Auto and travel (see instructions)	6			
7 Cleaning and maintenance	7			
8 Commissions	8			
9 Insurance	9	1,572		
10 Legal and other professional fees	10			
11 Management fees	11	3,562		
12 Mortgage interest paid to banks, etc. (see instructions)	12			
13 Other interest	13			
14 Repairs	14			
15 Supplies	15			
16 Taxes	16	2,503		
17 Utilities	17			
18 Depreciation expense or depletion	18	7,905		
19 Other (list) See Statement 4	19	2,136		
20 Total expenses. Add lines 5 through 19	20	17,678		
21 Subtract line 20 from line 3 (rents) and/or 4 (royalties). If result is a (loss), see instructions to find out if you must file Form 6198	21	4,522		
22 Deductible rental real estate loss after limitation, if any, on Form 8582 (see instructions)	22	1,656		

23a Total of all amounts reported on line 3 for all rental properties	23a	54,404	
b Total of all amounts reported on line 4 for all royalty properties	23b		
c Total of all amounts reported on line 12 for all properties	23c	744	
d Total of all amounts reported on line 18 for all properties	23d	40,688	
e Total of all amounts reported on line 20 for all properties	23e	75,480	
24 Income. Add positive amounts shown on line 21. Do not include any losses		24	4,955
25 Losses. Add royalty losses from line 21 and rental real estate losses from line 22. Enter total losses here		25	4,955
26 Total rental real estate and royalty income or (loss). Combine lines 24 and 25. Enter the result here. If Parts II, III, IV, and line 40 on page 2 do not apply to you, also enter this amount on Schedule 1 (Form 1040), line 5. Otherwise, include this amount in the total on line 41 on page 2		26	0

For Paperwork Reduction Act Notice, see the separate instructions.   Schedule E (Form 1040) 2022

GLOSSARY

1031 Exchange: A section of the U.S. Internal Revenue Service Code that allows investors to defer capital gains taxes on any exchange of like-kind properties for business or investment purposes.

Appreciation: An increase in the value of an asset over time. This increase can occur for a number of reasons, including increased demand or weakening supply, or as a result of changes in inflation or interest rates.

Asset: An item of ownership having exchange value.

Capital Gains: An increase in the value of a capital asset that gives it a higher worth than the purchase price. The gain is not realized until the asset is sold.

Debt to Income Ratio (DTI): A personal finance measure that compares an individual's debt payment to his or her overall income.

Depreciation: An accounting method of allocating the cost of a tangible asset over its useful life.

Interest: The charge for the privilege of borrowing money.

Home Equity Line of Credit (HELOC): A line of credit secured by your home that gives you a revolving credit line to use for larger expenses.

Home Owner's Association (HOA): An organization that makes and enforces rules and guidelines for the properties and residents of a subdivision, planned community, or condominium building/complex.

HVAC System: The heating, ventilation, and air conditioning system used to regulate the heating and cooling within a home.

LLC: A corporate structure whereby the members of the company cannot be held personally liable for the company's debts or liabilities.

Loan to Value: A lending risk assessment ratio that financial institutions and other lenders examine prior to approving a mortgage.

Net Worth: The amount by which your assets exceed your liabilities.

Origination Fee: An upfront fee charged by a lender to process a new loan application. The fee is compensation for executing the loan.

Processing: When your personal financial information is collected and verified to ensure all needed documentation is in place before your loan file is sent to underwriting.

Underwriting: The process a lender uses to determine if the risk of offering a mortgage loan to a borrower is acceptable to their investor, in order to issue a final approval on your loan.

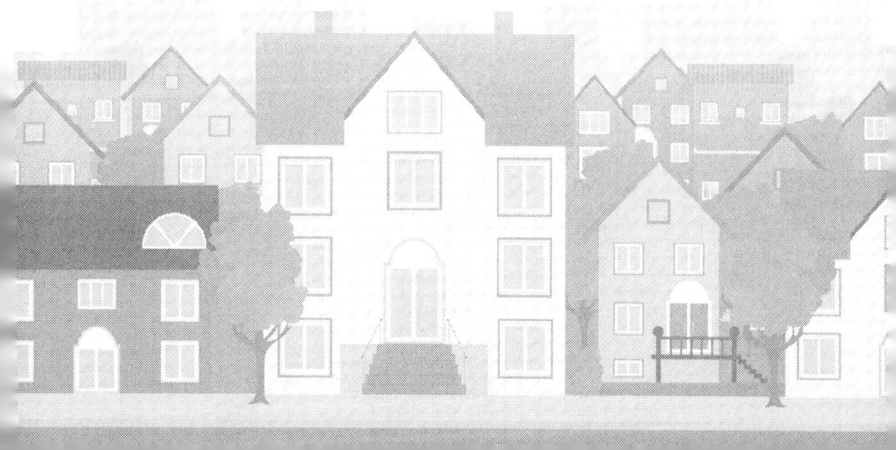

ABOUT THE AUTHOR:

Kathy Rex began her journey as a 1984 United States Air Force Academy (USAFA) Graduate in Management and as a member and co-captain of the 1988 Olympic Team Handball Squad. While serving in the Air Force and teaching at USAFA, she met Steve, her husband of 33 years, and raised three wonderful boys, Kobi, Kaci and Kyle. She used her acquired knowledge and leadership to successfully create and run the Landsharks Running Club for 20 years with her husband. For the past 6 years, Kathy has served as a home loan specialist at Churchill Mortgage and Bay Equity Home Loans. She loves the challenge of mentoring and assisting her clients through one of the largest investments in their lives.

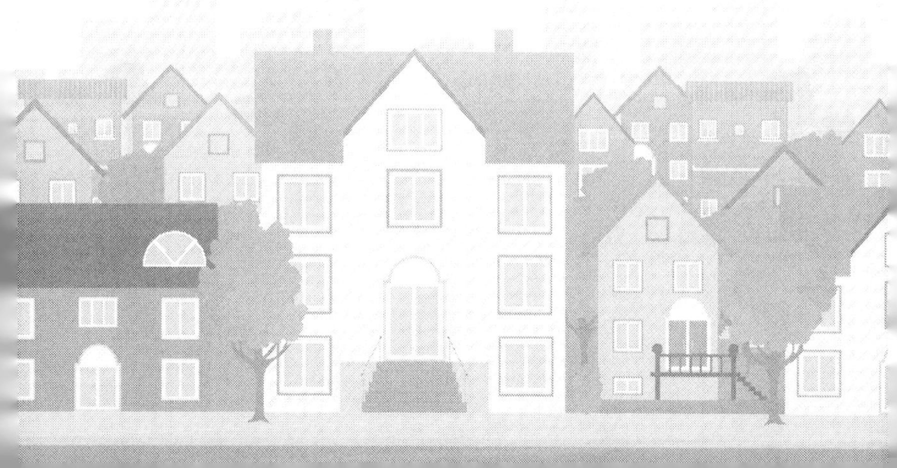

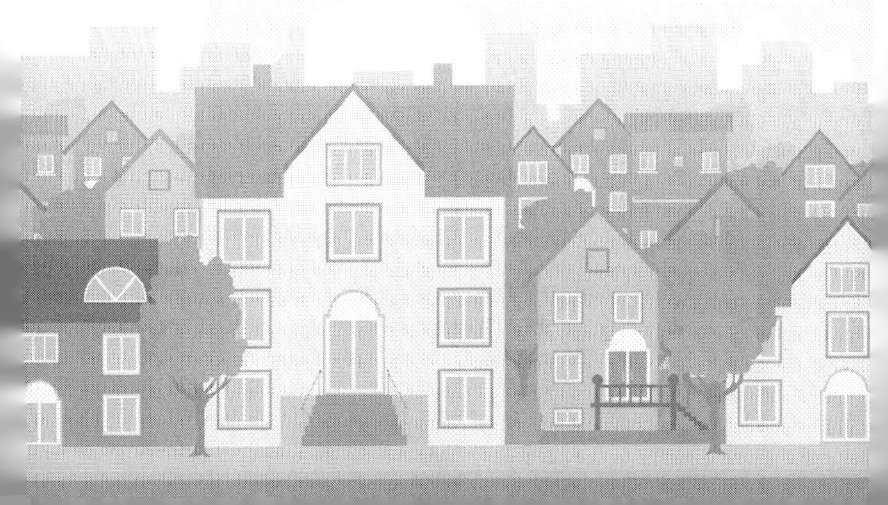

Made in the USA
Columbia, SC
01 October 2023